TIME OF DEATH

The true tale of a quest for justice
in 1960s Chapel Hill

NORA GASKIN

LYSTRA BOOKS
&c Literary Services

TIME OF DEATH: the true tale of a quest for justice in 1960s Chapel Hill
by Nora Gaskin

©2013 by Lystra Books & Literary Services.
391 Lystra Estates Drive
Chapel Hill, NC 27517

ISBN 978-0-9884164-5-1 paperbound
ISBN 978-0-9884164-2-0 ebook

Library of Congress Control Number: 2013942933

www.lystrabooks.com
lystrabooks@gmail.com

Book design by Kelly Prelipp Lojk
Author's photograph by Steven W. Esthimer, used with permission

FRANK J. RINALDI,
born March 15, 1929,
died Nov. 14, 2009

⤳

LUCILLE BEGG RINALDI,
born October 9, 1929,
died Dec. 24, 1963

(AUTHOR'S NOTE: *Two names, Stanley Forte's and Eddie Gorman's, have been changed to preserve their privacy.*)

DEC. 24, 1963, 8:45 A.M. Stanley Forte pulled up in front of friend Frank Rinaldi's house and honked the car horn. Frank came out and got in. "Together again, baby," Frank said and they set off, driving twelve miles or so from Chapel Hill to Durham, North Carolina, to go Christmas shopping.

They bought gifts for their wives, toys for Stan's two sons and Frank bought a teddy bear for the baby his wife, Lucille, was carrying.

When they returned to Frank's duplex apartment, 105 North Street, Chapel Hill, at about 1:30 p.m., they found that Lucille had been struck on the head, gagged, strangled and suffocated. She and her baby were both dead.

By 6 p.m., Frank was in jail, charged with murder.

⤳

THUS BEGAN AN ORDEAL THAT LASTED FOR TWO YEARS, AND A LIFETIME. Frank would be tried twice for the crime of murder. He was convicted in the first trial and spent a year in prison, held in seclusion on Death Row although he had not been sentenced to death. It was deemed to be for his safety.

FRANK WAS SUPPORTED BY A NUMBER OF FRIENDS, including my father, James Gaskin. Dad was a professor in the English Department at the University of North Carolina and he held a post in the graduate school that made him an advisor to graduate students. In both of those positions, he would have had a chance to know Frank. I have no reason to believe he was friendlier or closer to Frank than to others students, until Lucille died and Frank was arrested. My father always believed in Frank's innocence, and so did my mother, my sister, my brother and I. I was 12, almost 13, in December 1963, and for the next two years, my family life was led against the backdrop of the Rinaldi case. Dad was actively involved in supporting Frank, even visiting him as often as possible during the year he was in Central Prison.

My mother kept clippings from newspapers that covered the case. After both she and my dad died, I found the file and brought it home. I didn't read the clippings for quite a while because I was afraid to. As a grown-up, I knew that pregnant women who get murdered are most often murdered by the fathers of their babies. And I knew how rare a random murder is.

My dad never wavered on the question of Frank's innocence. I know that because I spoke with him about it late in his life. I feared that I would read the clippings and find doubt in my own mind. It wasn't doubt about Frank's innocence that worried me; it was doubt about my father's judgment.

I need not have feared. When I did read the clippings—not once but a number of times—I found that my own belief in Frank's innocence grew stronger and stronger. So did my desire to understand why he was arrested so quickly, why no real unbiased investigation took place and why an innocent man who was the victim of a terrible crime, and not the perpetrator, was convicted.

I believe that the case held up a mirror for my small and idealized hometown that found itself invaded by the larger world in the early and mid-1960s. The reflection wasn't pretty, but it has been compelling to me.

I have asked my sister for her remembrances and I have talked with Frank's good friend at the time, Kevin Kerrane. In April 2010, I had a conversation with Barry Winston, one of Frank's defense attorneys. Their recollections and the clippings have allowed me to put this story together.

FRANK RINALDI AND LUCILLE BEGG RINALDI both grew up in Waterbury, Connecticut. Their families lived near each other and he took her to her first high school prom in 1947. Frank went to prep school at the Taft School, then received his BA in English at Georgetown in 1951. He worked for the CIA for two years, including a stint in Paris, then joined the Army and served for three years. In 1956, he came to Chapel Hill and went to graduate school for a year. Then he took a teaching job at the University of Missouri, followed by a stay in Texas, a trip to Mexico, and a year or so in New York working for an advertising agency. In 1960, he returned to Chapel Hill and enrolled in the Ph.D. program in English.

Lucille seems to have stayed closer to home. She attended Albertus Magnus College in New Haven. In 1961, she received her masters degree in guidance at Fairfield University in Connecticut and afterward studied law for a year. She then began to work as a school teacher.

If Frank and Lucille maintained a friendship or romance through their 20s, it was long-distance, although they would have had opportunities to see each other when he visited his family and when he worked in New York.

Whether it was by long slow courtship or renewal of the high school attraction, they eventually made plans to marry.

They became engaged in the summer of 1962 and married on July 31, 1963.

They honeymooned at the Begg family's summer home on the coast of Connecticut, with Lucille's brother and his wife joining them for a weekend.

On Sept. 2, 1963, the newly-weds drove to Chapel Hill. But on Sept. 9, 1963, Lucille returned to Waterbury and resumed her job there.

She had planned to work at a junior high school in Chapel Hill, but found that the salary was substantially less than she had been earning and she was not pleased with the circumstances. She wrote to the principal that she was returning home due to a family emergency; when Frank was asked about it later, he said he believed she put it that way so as not to hurt any feelings, but that she was not happy with the new job.

When a bride returns home abruptly after a month of marriage, it could be a sign that the relationship is a troubled one. However, there is a wider context to consider that puts her departure in a different light.

Frank had been in Chapel Hill long enough to make good friends among his fellow graduate students, as well as with townspeople like Stan. They had met when Frank went to the Fortes' home with a woman friend of Mrs. Forte.

Frank lived in a graduate-student dorm for the 1962-63 academic year. Then, because he planned to marry Lucille at the end of July, he moved into an apartment on North Street. His Connor Dorm roommate and fellow English graduate student, Kevin Kerrane, shared the North Street apartment during the early part of the summer. Then Kevin went home to West Virginia. He was prepared to find a different place to live when he returned to Chapel Hill since he expected Lucille to be in residence on North Street. When she wasn't, he and another man named Jerry (last name not recalled) moved into the apartment to share expenses.

Frank and Kerrane were good friends, and Kevin was in a position to know a lot about Frank's personal life because they had shared accommodations for more than a year. Kevin saw no sign of trouble in the marriage. He remembers that Frank went to Connecticut or New York City to see Lucille regularly throughout the fall of 1963. The couple wrote letters and talked by telephone, and Frank spent Thanksgiving with Lucille in Waterbury. The only bit of unhappiness Kevin recalls is that Frank said Lucille's Aunt Lucy, with whom she lived that fall, was jealous of him and was unpleasant to him when he was in her home.

At 34, neither of the Rinaldis were children. They had known each other a long time. They had lived apart during their year-long engagement. Frank would not have expected to stay in Chapel Hill permanently; in fact, he could write his dissertation while living elsewhere. He would not have made much money teaching one freshman English course as a graduate instructor.

As for Lucille, she had lived as a single woman longer than many of her generation. She had a graduate degree and had explored law school. When she did marry, she left a job at which she was apparently good, where she was appreciated and relatively well-paid. It is possible Frank and Lucille agreed it made sense for her to go back to Waterbury to take up the job that was still open and for them to live as they had during their courtship; it would not be forever.

Lucille found herself pregnant—something that Kerrane says Frank was very excited about. After the murder on Christmas Eve, when Frank learned that the unborn child was a boy, he broke down. He told Kevin they had thought of naming a boy Christian. Frank's mother's maiden name was Christiano.

No doubt Lucille and Frank were making plans for their future, plans that they would not necessarily have shared with other people. In trial testimony, her family would say they were surprised when she and Frank became engaged. If true, that indicates that Lucille did not confide in them.

Lucille came to Chapel Hill on Dec. 20 for the Christmas holidays. Kerrane had borrowed Frank's car to drive home to West Virginia, and the third occupant of 105 North Street was also away. Frank and Lucille went to the Catholic Church for Sunday services, and Frank exchanged greetings with a man he knew only slightly, a young attorney, Barry Winston.

On Dec. 23, Stan Forte and his wife had dinner at the Rinaldis' apartment. It could be that the men made their plans for the next day then, or the shopping trip could have been planned further in advance. In the early and mid-60s, Chapel Hill's business district was made up of two or three blocks on Franklin Street. Most of the businesses catered to students, although there were two or three small family department stores and two nicer women's clothing stores. Eastgate Shopping Center, at the edge of town, had a mix of small shops and a grocery store. All in all, shopping opportunities in Chapel Hill were limited and many families with children—my own included—routinely went to the larger city of Durham. Northgate Mall was much larger than Eastgate, and downtown Durham was a vital shopping area with much more to offer than Chapel Hill. For the men to head toward Durham for Christmas shopping was not at all unusual or surprising.

Frank drove an attention-drawing car, a Lincoln that Lucille had found for him at an auction. It was an older model with the spare tire mounted on the back, and flashy enough for Frank to believe it appealed to women. He urged Kevin Kerrane to drive it on dates in order to impress the girl. But that car was not available to Frank and Stan Forte on December 24. Kevin had borrowed it for the holidays.

Anyone accustomed to seeing the Lincoln parked on North Street would have noticed that it had been gone for several days and may well have assumed that Frank himself was away and his apartment was empty. Chapel Hill's population dropped whenever the University was not in session.

THE TWO MEN HEADED FOR DURHAM in Stan's own distinctive car, a red and white Volkswagen Microbus. They went both to suburban Northgate Mall and the downtown shopping district, seeing people who remembered them or the Microbus. Later, they returned to Chapel Hill, stopping at Eastgate Shopping Center before going to Franklin Street, still shopping as they went. Again they saw people who could identify them. Trial testimony set up this timeline.

Stan Forte, driving his red and white VW Microbus, picked Frank up at approximately 8:45 a.m.

Stan stopped for gas at Jake's Sunoco on U.S. Route15-501, the highway to Durham. George Rhoton, who worked at the Sunoco, knew Stan and remembered seeing him at the station that morning. Mr. Rhoton also remembered the red and white Microbus. Mr. Rhoton said that there was a man with Stan. They were at the Sunoco at 9 and came from the direction of Chapel Hill. When the Microbus left the service station, it headed toward Durham. This was before drivers pumped their own gas. An attendant did it for you, so was in a position to testify.

Stan needed to stop by his insurance office at Northgate and Frank said he would go into the mall. Stan discovered that the office door was locked and the key was in his car. He started back to the car, saw Frank, and they went to Roses, a five-and-dime store. They spent some minutes in Roses looking for toy sword sets for Stan's sons, without luck.

They went to Kerr Rexall Drugstore to look for toys. The store didn't have the sword sets Stan wanted, and he talked to the manager, Julian Upchurch. Stan and Frank walked over to the lunch counter in Kerr Rexall and ordered coffee. Stan testified that they stayed there about 30 minutes.

Dave Hardy, one of Stan's colleagues, testified that he drank coffee with Stan and a man introduced to him as Frank Rinaldi on that Christmas Eve. Hardy said that it was about 9:30 a.m.

when they sat down, and he got up and left a few minutes after 10 to make a call.

As Hardy left, another colleague, Jack Hopkins, came in and took Hardy's seat at the booth. Hopkins testified that he, Stan and Frank stayed there for about 20 minutes. It was now about 10:30.

Stan still had paperwork to do, so Rinaldi went to Stan's office with him and waited for about 10 minutes while Stan did his work.

They then drove the Microbus and went to two stores on Broad Street in Durham looking for the sword sets, and after that, they drove to downtown Durham.

They went to Thalhimers Department Store where Stan bought gifts for his wife. Madge Spain, a clerk at Thalhimers, waited on Frank and assisted him in buying a maternity dress. She testified that he was there between 11 and 11:30. She remembered because she was to have gone to lunch at 11 but another clerk left first for lunch and Spain had to stay to wait on customers.

George Barrett, a man from Chapel Hill who ran the Storybook Farm day camp, was in Thalhimers that day and testified that he had seen Stan Forte—whom he knew because Stan's son had gone to the camp—with a man he [Barrett] didn't know.

Stan and Frank then went across the street to Woolworth's, made some purchases, and then went to another store where they didn't buy anything.

They drove the Microbus to Sears. Henry Semmer was at Sears and testified that he saw Frank—whom he knew—and a man he didn't know in Sears. His description of the man fit Stan Forte.

Stan and Frank drove back to Northgate and returned to Kerr Rexall. The manager, Julian Upchurch, was working the register because a clerk had gone to lunch. Frank checked out at Upchurch's register; the manager remembered because Frank had bought an artificial Christmas tree and Upchurch had to get a special cover for the tree. Upchurch remembered Stan Forte when he saw him again because of their early conversation about the toy swords. Upchurch "did not connect" that the two men were together.

Stan and Frank drove back to Chapel Hill and stopped at Eastgate Shopping Center for about 15 minutes. Stan went into three stores looking for a sewing set for his wife.

James Heavner, a Chapel Hill businessman, testified that he saw Stan Forte, with whom he was acquainted, at Eastgate at about 12:45. They greeted each other and shook hands.

Stan and Frank drove the Microbus to the shopping district on Franklin Street. Stan estimated this would have been at approximately 12:30 to 12:45. Stan stopped at the post office to check his mailbox. Frank waited in the car. Then Stan drove around to the Rosemary Street Merchants' Parking Lot so he could go into Pete the Tailor's and pick up a suit he'd left.

The two men went to Roses and to Huggins Hardware looking for the sewing set Stan wanted. Olga Hackett, who was working at Huggins that day, knew Frank and saw him in the store. She didn't remember the exact time; she thought it was before lunch. She also said she did not take a lunch break that day because the store was so busy. Based on other people's recollections, it seems likely that she had the time wrong—an honest mistake.

Stan and Frank went out the back door of the store, got into the Microbus and drove to Chapel Hill Tire on West Franklin. Stan estimated it was 1:05 p.m. He was planning a trip and wanted a new tire for the Microbus. The business was closed. Stan knocked on the door and Sion Jennings, the operator of the tire store, opened it. Mr. Jennings testified that he knew it was after 1 p.m. because he had closed the business at that hour so his employees could enjoy Christmas Eve. He knew Stan, and said that a man he didn't know was with him.

Stan and Frank drove to the North Street apartment, arriving there at about 1:30, and found Lucille.

WE KNOW MUCH LESS about how Lucille spent her last hours. Frank said later that they had eaten breakfast together and that she was writing a letter when he left home. Frank and Stan found her still wearing her pajamas and robe. We do know that she wrote at least one letter to a friend and that the letter was found in the apartment: "Frank has kissed and smiled his kisses and smiles and departed for Durham to tell Santa what a good girl I am," she had written. There is only one way to understand her words: She was alive when he left.

Earlier in the year of 1963, the county commissioners of Orange County (the county in which Chapel Hill is located) had budgeted for the county to hire a medical examiner to replace the elected coroner. However, as of Dec. 24, the position had not been filled. It was the elected coroner who happened to work at a funeral home who was called to examine Lucille's body. On advice from attorney, Barry Winston, Frank asked for an autopsy to be done by a pathologist at the university's medical school. Frank paid for the autopsy.

The pathologist determined that the body temperature showed Lucille had died no earlier than 10 a.m. and that "strangulation or asphyxiation" was the cause of death. The pathologist testified that she would not have died quickly—something sad to contemplate.

Thanks to television, many of us are amateur forensic scientists and psychologists these days. For a killer to have struck a victim over the head, tied a scarf over her mouth and nose and smothered her with a pillow suggests that the killer was not efficient and was perhaps not prepared to do what he or she did.

Once Frank was arrested on the evening of Dec. 24, he called the only attorney he knew, though only slightly. Barry Winston had joined the North Carolina bar in 1961. He had practiced in Atlanta before coming back to Chapel Hill, and he had been in his newly established practice for only a few weeks at the time of Lucille's death.

Frank told a reporter for the *Greensboro (NC) Daily News* he had seen Winston at church when he and Lucille attended together on Dec. 23. Winston did not remember that encounter, but he did remember meeting Frank earlier. He had bought a life insurance policy from Stan Forte and one day, walking down Franklin Street, he encountered Stan and a friend—Frank Rinaldi. Frank asked some questions about immigration law on behalf of friend; Winston could not answer the questions but remembered Frank.

Winston spent hours at the jail with Frank on the evening of the 24th. As he left, he pressed the police not to interview Frank in his absence. He also asked the police to take Frank to the university infirmary for a sedative. Records show that the police complied, but it is not known whether Frank took the medication he was given.

Even the people who were and are skeptical about Frank's innocence would have to acknowledge that his arrest was premature. No investigation had been done. No time had been taken to verify his and Stan's account of where they had been that day. No scientific information about the death was yet available, but Frank was in jail and stayed there.

A reporter, Roland Giduz, was given access to Frank and conducted an hour long interview on Thursday, Dec 26. Mr. Giduz' story appeared in the *Greensboro (NC) Daily News* on Friday, Dec. 27, 1963. He described Frank as "dazed but talking freely, [s]oft-spoken and bespectacled … [h]e appeared very weary, and chain-smoked cigarettes. He said he hadn't eaten anything since he and his wife had breakfast together on Christmas Eve." Giduz referred to an untouched package of food sent by friends. He asked Frank about a circulating story concerning a bloody shirt; Frank declined to answer on advice of his attorney.

When I interviewed Barry Winston in April 2010, I asked if he knew about the newspaper interview when it was conducted. He was very clear: He did not and he would not have allowed it. It was contradictory to requests he had made to the police that night. He also said that it probably didn't harm Frank's case. He had no recollection about a bloody shirt, nor is it mentioned in any other newspaper accounts.

To quote further from Giduz' article: "[Barry] Winston said he would give Chapel Hill police the autopsy report 'as soon as we resolve an impasse we seem to have reached in communications. I cannot get any information from the police about this case,' he added. 'We want to know what makes them think my client is the man they want.'" Indeed.

Roland Giduz quoted police Chief William Blake in the Dec. 27 article: "A lot of loose ends need to be put together in the investigation, such as the motive, time of death and cause of death."

Reading that now, I scratch my head and wonder just what they did have and why they focused on Frank so soon and so completely.

A PROBABLE-CAUSE HEARING was held in early Jan. 1964. Stan Forte was one of the witnesses who testified at the hearing. Kevin Kerrane was not there, but several other graduate students attended in support of Frank. Stan was asked what Frank had said when he got into Stan's car on Christmas Eve morning. "Together again, baby," Stan answered. Frank's graduate-student friends were glad to hear those words. To them, it was pure Frank—a characteristic thing for him to say. For those who believed in his innocence, they thought this lighthearted greeting made it clear that he could not be a coldblooded killer. Ultimately that greeting would be used against Frank with devastating effect.

With corroboration for Frank's alibi, the pathologist's report, and with Lucille's letter—"Frank departed for Durham"—a judge ruled that there was no probable cause to hold Frank for the murder.

At the probable-cause hearing, the time and cause of death were no longer "loose ends." The time of death and the alibi witnesses would seem to make it impossible for Frank to have committed the murder. However, the Chapel Hill police and the State Bureau of Investigation were convinced that he was their man and they continued to investigate him to the exclusion of everyone else.

Why? This remains a compelling question. In my cozy hometown, a town in which there was one economic and moral force—the university—how could a man stunned by grief after discovering his dead wife and unborn child be arrested just hours later, with no evidence at all? Why, to use a more current phrase, the rush to judgment?

And why would investigators not at least allow for the possibility that they could be wrong? After all, if they were, a killer would go free.

A month and two days before Lucille and her baby died, the president of the United States had been assassinated. Then we had watched on television as his accused killer was murdered while in police custody. The earth was shifting under our feet and we were frightened.

The Civil Rights movement had also come to Chapel Hill. Segregationists were disturbed because their principles were being rejected in the larger world, and now up and down Franklin Street itself. There were marches, demonstrations, sit-ins and violence. (John Ehle's brilliant book, THE FREE MEN, describes the impact of demonstrations on Chapel Hill.)

Other white residents cherished the town's liberal reputation. Now the limits on the town's—and their own—liberalness were exposed. The town's confidence that it was superior to places like Birmingham was shaken.

Against the background of change, uncertainty and fear, it was simply not acceptable for a crime like Lucille Rinaldi's murder to happen. When it did occur, no time could be lost in nailing a suspect and her husband would do. Once this stand was taken by the police and the State Bureau of Investigation, it had to be defended. The judge's dismissal of the case due to lack of evidence meant that evidence had to be patched together.

During the spring of 1964, police officers, including Detective Howard Pendergraph, and SBI agents Frank Satterfield and Hayward Starling set about to talk to Frank's friends and investigate his life. Kevin Kerrane remembered that a police officer came on to a very attractive female graduate student he was interviewing. She and her friends were appalled by the officer's behavior and lack of professionalism.

Since Kerrane had lived with Frank Rinaldi, what he had to say was important. Agent Satterfield and a police officer interviewed him and asked him who else had a key to the apartment. Kerrane and Frank had moved into the apartment at the end of the previous academic year, in May or June of 1963. They had hired a handyman to clean the apartment and help them get moved in. For several days, the handyman, Eddie Gorman, had had a key and Kerrane told the investigators so. He remembers that Agent Satterfield wrote it down, asking how to spell Eddie's name.

Gorman did odd jobs around town, just as he had for Frank and Kevin. He also worked as a waiter at a restaurant called the Zoom Zoom. He seems to have been in no trouble with the law but Kerrane thought he was a bit of a shady character. Frank had told Kerrane that Gorman offered to sell him a television set at a low price and Frank turned it down, suspecting that it could have been stolen.

At the time Kerrane told the officers Gorman's name, he had a sense that they had not heard it before in connection to the case, but before long Eddie Gorman became well known in Chapel Hill.

EDDIE GORMAN TOLD THE POLICE that Frank Rinaldi had offered him money to kill Lucille, that he—Gorman—saw Frank at Eastgate on Christmas Eve and Frank ran over to him, calling, "It's over Eddie. I did it" or words to that effect.

Gorman's story was dramatic, but it didn't give the investigators a motive. They thought they found one when they discovered that Frank had purchased a $20,000 double-indemnity life insurance policy on Lucille weeks before they were married. He had purchased a $10,000 policy on himself at the same time. With Lucille murdered, he stood to get $40,000. Unless he was convicted of killing her himself.

Money is one of the classic motives for murder. The other is sex, and Eddie Gorman also told the police that Frank had made sexual advances toward him. At the time, this was secret, dark, hidden and shameful sex. Evidence was not needed. The shocking innuendo of homosexuality would do.

Was Frank homosexual? Kevin Kerrane said he thought not. Frank was engaged to Lucille when Kevin met him. He knew of one heterosexual encounter that Frank had, other than with Lucille. Also, Kevin had a serious girlfriend when he and Frank first met and Frank had encouraged the relationship until it ended. Frank had offered the loan of his flashy car when Kevin wanted to impress a girl. When Kevin began dating the woman who became his wife, Frank was again encouraging. That woman, Sheila, liked Frank, as did a number of other women who were friends.

None of the above precludes Frank from being homosexual. In his contemporary reporting on the trial, Perry Young does not say explicitly that the prosecution offered any corroboration of Gorman's allegations about sexual advances. The reports do mention a postcard that was taken from Frank's apartment but was not admitted into evidence. In his article published in the *Independent Weekly* on August 13, 2003, Young recalled more about the postcard. He said it contained the words "pansies" and "fruits." He also recalled the young man who wrote the postcard being "grilled" on the stand by Cooper. In his articles written at the time of the trial, Young did not shy away from discussion of sexuality as it came out in court, or the sexual language that went with it, yet the contents of the postcard were not quoted. Perhaps he sought to minimize the impact on a witness who did nothing more than write a postcard. Perhaps Cooper's grilling of the witness was one of the several blind side sneak attacks the solicitor made.

In addition to money and sex, Eddie Gorman brought yet another social vibration that the prosecution could exploit. Eddie Gorman was black. In a town where a liberal reputation was being tarnished, there was pressure to believe Eddie because of his race. A girl who had been my close friend since first grade called me a racist because I did not believe Gorman.

Over the spring and summer of 1964, the police and SBI investigation did their work and County Solicitor Thomas D. Cooper took what they had gathered to the grand jury. As a result, in August Frank was indicted and charged with Lucille's murder.

THE FIRST TRIAL BEGAN ON MONDAY, NOV. 9, 1964. *The Chapel Hill (NC) Weekly* was published twice a week, on Wednesdays and Sundays. In his 2003 piece written for the *Independent Weekly* (Durham, NC), Perry Deane Young recalled covering the trial as a young reporter. He wrote, "I was working for the legendary editor, Jim Shumaker, at *The Chapel Hill (NC) Weekly* and he gave me free rein covering this very sensational trial. We all but ran a full transcript of each day's proceedings, taking up whole pages of the newspaper."

It is fortunate that Shumaker allowed the coverage and that a writer with Young's talent covered the case. His stories are compelling reading.

In an article for *The Chapel Hill Weekly*, Wednesday, Nov. 11, 1964, Young set the scene in the courtroom. Frank's father, brother and uncle had come from Connecticut. They sat behind Frank, "stiff and solemn ... The family and friends of the late Mrs. Lucille Begg Rinaldi are more talkative, more responsive and more stylish than the Rinaldis." Lucille's brother and his wife, father and stepmother, and two friends were there. Lucille's brother was a lawyer and "on the second day sat inside the bar, just behind the solicitor and conferred with the prosecution on the jurors."

The Begg family believed that Frank was guilty. Kevin Kerrane said that they learned of Lucille's death when they got a call from the Chapel Hill police department. The police also told them that Frank had been arrested and kept the Beggs apprised of their theories of the crime.

The presiding judge was the Honorable Raymond Mallard. Frank was represented by two attorneys, Barry Winston and Gordon Battle.

A venire of 36 prospective jurors was called. Apparently 20 of them were dismissed quickly, leaving 16 who were sworn in. Then, in what seems a hopelessly outdated procedure even then, a 5-year-old boy was brought in to draw the jurors' names out of a cigar box. That drawing determined what jurors were to be sworn in a second time and questioned in voir dire.

Cooper could issue six challenges without cause. The defense could challenge 14. The judge could dismiss an indefinite number for cause.

The solicitor asked each candidate for biographical information, whether or not he or she had followed the case in the newspapers, whether he or she knew Frank or Lucille or Stanley Forte. He also asked about connections to the university and whether Frank's employment there would have an influence on his or her decisions.

The solicitor allowed four people who said they were opposed to capital punishment to be seated, interpreted by Perry Young to mean that Cooper did not plan to seek the death penalty.

Three jurors were seated before the midday break at 1p.m. Three more were seated during the afternoon and the original jury pool was exhausted. The judge ordered that another 125 names be called.

On Tuesday morning, 5 people were seated. After lunch, the 12th person was seated. The judge ordered that two alternates be selected instead of the usual one.

Of note: Eighteen people were dismissed for cause because they had formed the opinion that Frank was guilty. And Frank had to stand to hear the indictment charging that he had murdered his wife, read twice on Tuesday afternoon.

The jury was made up of nine men and three women. The alternates were one woman and one man. None worked for the university, although one man had a wife who worked as a secretary in the psychology department. One of the jurors, a woman, was identified as "a negro," as was the man chosen as an alternate.

Chapel Hill is a university town and university people accept transience. My father lived there for almost 50 years before his death and my mother for 45; I live here still and have friends here who I've known since kindergarten or earlier. However, as stable as long-timers may be, we are the exception and we didn't grow up expecting to stay put. Going through public schools, our teachers often left after two or three years as their graduate-student spouses received their degrees and moved on. Friends moved away when their parents' graduated from one of the professional schools. I was used to knowing people from all over the United States and the world. But Solicitor Cooper made sure the jurors were not university people. Besides Chapel Hill, they came from Hillsborough, Rougemont, and unincorporated parts of rural Orange County. I speculate that in many of their eyes, Frank—a Yankee, a man who had lived in Europe and Missouri and New York, who had been in the CIA—was an outsider, or as the saying goes, "not from here." Perhaps that played a role in the way the police pursued him, too. Cooper, no doubt, counted on it as he set about to portray Frank as a certain "kind of man."

On Wednesday, Nov. 11, 1964, the case in chief began. The defense immediately made a motion to suppress all physical evidence taken from Frank's apartment on Dec. 24, 1963. Young's article quoted from the motion at length. "Now comes the defendant, Frank Joseph Rinaldi, and respectfully moves the Court to suppress evidence obtained by agents of the Chapel Hill Police Department and the North Carolina State Bureau of Investigation from his person and from his residence at 105 North Street, Chapel Hill, North Carolina on December 24, 1963, and subsequent thereto; for that said evidence was obtained under an illegal search or searches in violation of the defendant's rights under the laws and constitution of North Carolina, and the Constitution and amendments thereto of the United States. The defendant further moves the Court that all personal property obtained by said illegal search or searches be forthwith returned."

The jury had been seated in the courtroom and when this motion was made—taking Solicitor Cooper by surprise—it had to be excused so that a hearing could be held.

According to Perry Young's story, the solicitor acknowledged that there was no search warrant, but that the search and arrest were justified because the investigators had grounds to believe a murder had been committed. Detective Pendergraph testified that he had taken a pocketbook, letters that were in the pocketbook and pencils from the apartment. Agent Satterfield testified that he also took letters and papers, some of which were taken to the SBI offices so that photo copies could be made.

All documents were then turned over the Chapel Hill Police Department.

Defense attorneys asked Satterfield about a postcard addressed to Frank, and about which he had questioned a man named Charles Gattis. Satterfield said he had seen a copy but had not seen the original.

SBI Agent Starling listed "articles" he had taken from the apartment, which remained in SBI custody.

The judge ruled that items taken from the apartment should be returned to Frank, and they were, in open court. They included a flashlight with two dents in it and a bloody pillow. Barry Winston remembers the flashlight and a partial fingerprint on it. The print could not be matched to Frank's. Perry Young reported that the police did not test the apartment for finger prints.

IN THE SUNDAY, NOV. 15, 1964 edition of the *Chapel Hill (NC) Weekly*, Young covered the testimony of Lucille's family members. Lucille's aunt, Lucy Begg, took the stand. She said that while the Rinaldis lived just a few doors down from the Beggs in Waterbury, the Rinaldi sons went to public school and the Beggs went to parochial school. (Note: Frank Rinaldi's obituary states that he went to the private Taft School for high school.) Frank did take Lucille to her senior prom in 1947 but then they went to colleges in different states. They did see each other on holidays, and Frank gave Lucille an engagement ring for Christmas in 1962. Miss Begg said that it was on that Christmas Eve that Frank met Lucille's family. If that is so, it seems that Lucille did not necessarily confide in her family. If it isn't true, it shows Miss Begg's antipathy toward Frank.

Clara Begg, married to Lucille's brother, William Jr., also testified. The Begg family had a vacation home in Wilford, CT. Following their July 31, 1963 wedding, Frank and Lucille used it for the first 10 days of August. Clara and Bill Jr., visited them for a weekend, and Clara told in court about a conversation she had with Frank while "Cille" and Bill were swimming. Clara said that Frank had said to her "Look at them out there. She's probably discussing all my bad faults ... saying she married me because she felt sorry for me ... and I'm not good enough ..."

Clara Begg told the jury that Frank had told her he had put Lucille in an awkward position the night before by asking her about her share of the family property and asking was he not part owner as well? He then asked Clara about Lucille's claim to property. Lucille and Bill were coming close to where Clara and Frank were sitting and Frank signaled to Clara not to mention the topic of property.

The Beggs' testimony was meant to be detrimental to Frank; they were prosecution witnesses and they believed that Frank killed Lucille. Reading and rereading Young's version of the testimony one wonders how much Lucy and Clara's feelings about Frank shaped their recollections. Frank hardly knew Clara and Bill that day at the coast, and they hardly knew him. They certainly could have been awkward with each other. Frank was known to have a self-deprecating sense of humor that his new in-laws didn't know how to take, or, after the fact, throwaway statements could have been reinterpreted as sinister. In any event, none of their testimony rises to the standard of evidence of murder. But it does fit into the picture of a man concerned with money that the solicitor wanted to create.

On Sept. 2, 1963, Frank and Lucille had headed for Chapel Hill. Frank's distinctive but unreliable Lincoln was not roadworthy so he left it in Waterbury to be repaired. The plan was for Aunt Lucy to call when it was ready.

Young's article does not say how they traveled, but it seems they were driving a car other than Frank's. They stopped in Henderson, NC to visit Frank's friends, the Hicks family. Frank often stopped to see the Hickses when he drove to and from Connecticut. Jasper

Hicks testified to the visit and said it lasted about an hour before Frank and Lucille continued on to Chapel Hill.

The next witness was the Chapel Hill school superintendent, Howard Thompson, who said that Lucille had signed a contract for the 1963-64 school year and attended two days of teachers' meetings but did not appear at work on the first day of class, Sept. 9.

Frank and Lucille drove through the night of Sept. 8 and 9 and arrived at Frank's parents' house at 4 a.m. Testimony about the trip and arrival came from Lucy Begg when she was on the stand. Lucille and Frank slept at the Rinaldis' for much of the day, then went to see Lucy at her office at 5 in the afternoon. Lucille told her aunt that she had driven the whole way from North Carolina while Frank slept. Begg described her niece as being in "very poor condition." She said that Frank told her, by way of explanation, that Lucille didn't like his friends in Chapel Hill or "just didn't get along with his way of living and that maybe she ought to go into a convent."

We have only Begg's word as to what was said, and it was only her interpretation.

Lucy Begg said that the couple had stayed in Waterbury, alternating between her house and Frank's parents' for two weeks until his car was fixed and he could return to Chapel Hill. Then Lucille stayed at her aunt's house through the fall.

Lucy Begg testified that Frank did not send Lucille a card for her birthday on Oct. 9. He had called but missed her because she had gone to his brother and sister-in-law's house for birthday cake. Lucy Begg said that Lucille went to New York to meet Frank once and that he was four hours late arriving. Begg did acknowledge that the husband and wife wrote to each other and called each other during the fall.

Frank joined Lucille in Waterbury at Thanksgiving and they stayed with his parents. Aunt Lucy Begg invited the couple to dinner but said that Frank would not eat at the table with her and did not speak to her. "I was in his presence, but he completely ignored me ... I knew something was wrong."

We have the testimony of a grief-stricken aunt against the man she believed murdered her niece. Then there was my conversation with Kevin Kerrane in Nov. 2009. He saw Frank everyday in Chapel Hill during the fall of 1963 and, other than the unconventional arrangement for newlyweds, saw nothing that indicated that the marriage was troubled, although he did remember that Frank said Aunt Lucy was jealous of him.

By Thanksgiving, Lucille would have known she was pregnant. In Mr. Young's account of trial testimony, there is no mention of the pregnancy from either Lucy Begg or Clara Begg. Why weren't they asked about it?

On Dec. 20, 1963, Lucille took a train from New Haven to North Carolina. On Dec. 22, Lucille and Frank went to church. On Dec. 23, a Monday, Stan Forte and one of his two sons stopped by 105 North Street for a brief visit. Later, Stan, his wife and both sons came to supper at the Rinaldis' apartment and the next day, Stan and Frank went to Durham to shop, getting back to find Lucille at about 1:30 or 1:35.

Police Captain Coy Durham testified in a statement taken on the day of murder that Stan said they returned to the apartment at about 2. Captain Durham also said that Stan had told him, "Mr. Rinaldi reached into his mailbox, then put his key in the door and the minute he opened the door he said: 'Oh my God, somebody's killed and robbed my wife.'"

As one might guess, the time that the two men returned to the apartment and the time of the murder was important; a half hour or 25-minute discrepancy in Stan's testimony mattered.

Detective Howard Pendergraph was in charge of the investigation of Lucille's death. He testified that he had checked all of the doors and windows at 105 North Street and found no sign of forced entry. On cross-examination, Barry Winston asked Pendergraph if he had gone into the attic. He said that he had opened the pull-down attic steps, went up, and looked around but did not go into it. Mr. Winston pointed out that the attic was accessible from both sides of the duplex; had Detective Pendergraph examined the doors and windows of the other apartment? He had not.

The state called two witnesses to speak as to Frank Rinaldi's whereabouts on Dec. 24, 1963. The first was Olga Hackett who worked at Huggins Hardware Store and knew Frank. It was she who put Frank in Chapel Hill "before lunch," although it is likely she was mistaken about the time.

EDDIE GORMAN WAS THE STAR WITNESS. In a hearing held in August, Gorman had said that he saw Frank at Eastgate at approximately 11:30 or noon on the 24th. On the witness stand during the trial, he said it was noon or 1 p.m. Gorman testified that when he and Frank saw each other at Eastgate, Frank called out "Eddie, it's over. I did it," or similar words. Later, Stan Forte would say that he and Frank were together all of the time that they were at Eastgate and that he, Stan, did not see Gorman.

Of course, Gorman's most important testimony was that Frank had made homosexual advances toward him and that Frank on several occasions offered him money to kill Lucille.

Eddie Gorman said that he had told two people about Frank's offer of money to kill his wife. Those two people also testified. One of them, Victor Young, was a student who worked part time at the Zoom Zoom with Eddie. Victor Young said that Rinaldi "bothered" Gorman by calling frequently and coming by the restaurant. When Young asked Gorman about it, Gorman told him that Frank wanted to hire him to kill his wife. Victor said that the conversation took place sometime before Thanksgiving 1963.

Kenneth Putnam was the manager of the Zoom Zoom. He testified that somebody had come to the restaurant to see Eddie one night but "had his back to him and he couldn't tell who it was. 'I figured it was somebody wanting money,' Mr. Putnam testified and so he asked Eddie about it. Eddie told him 'He asked me to help kill his wife.' Mr. Putnam said, 'I said "you're kidding" and passed it off. Mr. Putnam reported the conversation to police after he had heard about Lucille's death."

There is no way of assessing Eddie Gorman's truthfulness about anything he said to anyone, or whether or not the man Putnam saw talking to him was in fact Frank Rinaldi.

Dr. Nathaniel Rodman, the pathologist who had performed the Christmas Eve autopsy testified that, based on body temperature, the time of death was between 10 a.m. and 5 p.m. Since Lucille's body had been found at about 1:30 or 2 it was nonsensical to say the time of death could have been later than that. It was not gracefully delivered expert testimony.

Before resting, the state also introduced testimony that Frank had borrowed $752.24 from a local bank on Nov. 1, 1963 and had applied for a $2,300 student loan earlier that fall. On the application, Frank had said that $750 would be used to pay for life insurance. The University approved a loan of $800 on Oct. 22.

The prosecution also introduced a photostat of a postcard written to Frank from a male friend. The defense protested and the judge suppressed it. However, the copy had been identified before the defense objected.

Of course, the prosecution did not introduce the letter Lucille had written after Frank left home on Christmas Eve morning. I asked Barry Winston how they had kept it out. He said that the letter was in his possession; to be sure it didn't get mislaid, he punched holes in it and put it in a notebook. Because of the holes, the police refused to agree that it was the same note that was found on the date of death. Kevin Kerrane remembers Winston asking if it was the same, except for the holes. The prosecution objected and the judge sustained the objection, and the letter was out.

The prosecution rested at 11:37 a.m. on Friday, Nov. 13, 1964.

THE DEFENSE'S GOAL would have been to show that the prosecution's case did not erase reasonable doubt that Frank had killed Lucille. Besides the obvious ways in which this was true, Barry Winston and Gordon Battle must have felt that their client's actual innocence would be evident. But the fact that he had been charged and was on trial meant that they to work hard.

One of the defense witnesses was the court reporter who had worked at the Christmas Eve preliminary hearing. Detective Pendergraph had testified at that hearing and Barry Winston had the reporter's transcript read into the trial record. On Christmas Eve, the detective had said that he checked two out of eight windows for evidence of a break-in, and that the bathroom window had no lock.

A man named Curtis Woodlief who worked for the funeral home that took Lucille's body to the hospital, testified about the state of rigor mortis he had found when he moved her body. With that testimony on record, Barry Winston recalled Dr. Rodman and asked if, knowing the degree of rigor mortis, he could further refine the time of death. Yes, Dr. Rodman said, he could: Lucille died between 10 a.m. and noon.

The defense then called a series of witnesses who could testify to having seen Frank and Stan while they were shopping, from 8:45 a.m. until they found Lucille at about 1:30 p.m. They are the witnesses who, collectively, provided the timeline for the morning of the murder.

The defense's most important witness was Stanley Forte. He was on the stand when court adjourned for the day.

THE NEXT ISSUE OF THE CHAPEL HILL (NC) WEEKLY, Wednesday, Nov. 18, 1964, had a banner headline: JURY FINDS RINALDI GUILTY. A lot had happened in three days. Again, the story was written by Perry Young.

On Monday, Stanley Forte had resumed his testimony for the defense. The following is an excerpt from the news story in *The Chapel Hill Weekly* regarding Forte's testimony: "We pulled up in front of the apartment ... Frank got out ... I got out, and went behind Frank. We entered the vestibule. He was standing directly in front of the door to his apartment," Forte testified. "He reached into the mail box to the left of the door. He pulled out his mail ... including a Christmas card I had mailed him.

"He [Rinaldi] opened the door ... we both looked into the apartment and saw the scene. Lucille was lying on the floor, face down, her head slightly tilted to the right ... her pocketbook was on the floor to her left ... her feet were toward the door," he testified. "Her arms were under her, in front of her thighs. Part of the contents of the pocketbook were on the floor. Items from the table were on the floor ... a lamp was overturned.

"I went to Lucille, knelt down beside her. I removed her hand from her right side and felt of the wrist. I reached toward her head. There was a knot in a scarf around her head. I untied that knot and got up and went directly to the phone and called the Chapel Hill Police Department ... I know the time was 1:40 because I looked at the clock that was there.

"Forte said Rinaldi started 'mumbling incoherently' when he saw his wife's body. He further testified that Rinaldi got behind him and 'nudged' him into the room.

"On cross-examination, Forte was asked what Rinaldi said when he first got into the car that morning. He said Rinaldi said, 'Together again, baby.'

"Cooper asked if there was any particular significance to the term 'baby.' 'We were good friends,' Forte replied. Cooper asked another question about the term and Forte said it was 'a common term.' Cooper then asked 'among men?' Forte said 'yes.' To this, the solicitor offered an aside: 'That's in the crowd that you and Frank run around with.'

"Also in cross-examination, Cooper asked Forte if Rinaldi were ever in the CIA. Forte said yes, but that he did not know Rinaldi was suspended for security reasons."

The reason why Forte didn't know about the suspension for security reasons is that it did not happen. Consider that Frank served in the military after his years in the CIA. Does the military take people who are deemed security risks by the CIA? It seems that this hit-and-run form of question on the part of Cooper was intended to imply that Frank was a security risk because he was homosexual. The defense was not prepared to counter.

As noted before, when Frank bought the $20,000 life insurance policy on Lucille, he bought a $10,000 policy on himself. Eventually, Cooper made the point that Frank had bought a smaller policy for himself than for his wife; Stan Forte testified that Frank already had another $10,000 policy on his own life.

People continue to find Lucille's insurance policy to be a problem when they look at the case. I do not.

Lucille was to be the breadwinner in the marriage until Frank finished his degree and had a job. A number of teachers in the Chapel Hill-Carrboro public schools were working to put spouses through graduate or professional school. The teachers were always the wives. In the schools at the time, this was considered normal but to the jury, this may have been an unusual idea. Perhaps that was Mr. Cooper's hope.

I worked as a financial advisor for more than 24 years. By the time I began that career in 1981, we had many investment vehicles available, and many more now, but based on my experience, quite a few people continue to view life insurance policies that build cash value as investment vehicles. In earlier decades, this was even truer. Certainly insurance companies have marketed them that way for more than a century. Frank and Lucille may have felt that the policies they were buying were for their future.

They bought the policies through Frank's good friend, Stanley Forte, and they may have wanted to help him in his career.

Frank already had other life insurance and which explains the discrepancy between the $20,000 policy on Lucille as compared to a lower amount on him. Lucille signed the application for the contract, so was fully aware of its purchase.

Apparently, Frank's policy bought at the same time as Lucille's was canceled because of false statements on the application. Cooper asked Stan Forte, the insurance agent who sold the policies, if he knew that Frank was undergoing psychiatric treatment when he made application. Stan said he did not know.

From Young's article, it does not appear that Cooper offered other information on Frank's mental health history. This seems to be another hit-and-run, with an impression made but not quite presented as fact and not corroborated.

Cooper then went on to sideswipe Stan's own character. He brought out that a postal inspector had once questioned Forte about literature that Forte said "might be classified" as obscene or pornographic. Stan denied that he told the inspector he was doing research for a master's thesis. He also denied that he had possessed a photograph of a woman being strangled. Apparently Stan had declined to take a lie-detector test on the subject of the mail; the court did not allow Cooper to ask about that.

Cooper asked Forte if Frank was homosexual. The defense objected and the objection was sustained, so Cooper asked if Frank had ever made advances to Stan Forte, or if Stan had ever made advances to Frank. The answer was "Absolutely not." For what good that would do. The word "homosexual" could not be unsaid.

Stan did acknowledge that Frank had applied for the $40,000 life insurance benefit from Lucille's double indemnity policy. Considering that Frank had two attorneys to pay and had hired a private investigator, it is not surprising that he would try to access what money he could, and was entitled to.

Quoting Young again: "Another surprise question from the State was, 'Did you put Lucille Rinaldi's body in that car before you left for Durham?'"

It is difficult to imagine what Cooper was getting at, except to ask one last inflammatory question without offering anything to substantiate it.

The defense rested at 3:10 p.m. on Monday, Nov. 16. Court adjourned until the next day.

THE DEFENSE GAVE ITS CLOSING ARGUMENTS FIRST, with Barry Winston beginning. He talked for 50 minutes. He told the jury that the state had presented "red herrings, smoke rings [sic] and smears." He pointed out that the introduction of homosexuality especially was unsupported. "Did the State have evidence? I suggest to you the State brought this up because it had nothing else."

Winston mocked Eddie Gorman's believability and pointed out discrepancies between statements he had made at different times. How likely was it that Frank Rinaldi asked Eddie 12 times or more to kill Lucille? How likely was it that Frank ran up to Eddie in a crowded shopping center, calling "It's over. I did it"?

The defense attorney took care not to say that law enforcement officers lied, but he called into question Captain Durham's memory of the crime scene, which had been faulty, and reminded the jurors that Detective Pendergraph had not done a thorough job of checking the apartment for break-ins, and had testified differently about it. Perry Young doesn't mention it, but one presumes Winston reminded the jury that no fingerprints were taken.

"One thing is certain," Winston concluded to the jury. "When you've cut away the red herrings, the smoke screens and the smear attempts, the State has failed to prove beyond a reasonable doubt that Frank Rinaldi killed his wife … they have not even shown he could have done it."

Gordon Battle, the second defense attorney, began by defining "verdict" for the jury, coming from Latin, meaning "to tell the truth." He told the jury that only they could decide the truth, and that if they made a mistake, it could not be corrected.

He went on to attack the credibility of Eddie Gorman and said that Eddie could have killed Lucille.

Gorman knew the apartment, had once had a key he could have copied, but whether or not he did copy it, he probably knew that the bathroom window had no lock. And he would have known Frank's car. He could have observed that the car was gone and assumed that this meant the apartment was empty for the holidays. If he went in to rob it, Lucille would have surprised him and he could have attacked her in a disorganized, unplanned way that added to the brutality.

Barry Winston told me in 2010 that he believes Gorman committed the murder. I am neutral: As rare as random crime is, it does occur. One need not think Eddie Gorman was guilty to see that his existence and the failure of the police to investigate him—or anyone other than Frank—creates reasonable doubt.

Battle took his argument in a different direction. He challenged the jury: Did his suggestion that Eddie did it make the jurors angry? "I think it should," he said. "By the same token, it makes me mad that the State of North Carolina contends Frank Rinaldi did it … they have no proof of that." He attacked Eddie: He could not keep a job; he didn't live with his wife; he bought a car and it was repossessed a month later; he could not remember where the alleged sexual advances Frank made took place because, Battle said, they didn't happen. "'When you're telling the truth, it's not nearly so hard to keep things straight. But a liar can't remember what he said fifteen minutes before … because you've got to remember what you lied. Mr. Gorman hasn't done a very good job of it.'"

He offered an explanation of what Frank could have meant if he had spoken to Eddie at Eastgate: He, Frank, had cleaned the apartment. Battle reinforced that the State had offered no evidence of homosexuality on Frank's part.

Gordon Battle ended: "[T]here isn't anything you or anybody else can do to bring back Frank Rinaldi's wife or give birth to that unborn child ... there are scars on him, from the spotlight of publicity that will be with him for life. Let your verdict ring out that in North Carolina we do not kill a man or send him to prison on the type of evidence here."

SOLICITOR COOPER gave his chronology of Frank's life. He focused on the life insurance, Frank's relationship with Lucille, and his "attachment" to men. He found fault with Frank's failure to push Stan out of the way and run to Lucille's side. He characterized Stan Forte as a pornographer who did not cooperate with the police. He pointed out that Eddie Gorman had no criminal record. He sneered at the use of the term "baby." In fact, in Perry Deane Young's 2003 *Independent Weekly* article, he recalls that the solicitor used the word "baby" 15 times in his closing argument.

Cooper offered the jury a choice of four times when Frank had an opportunity to kill Lucille. It could have been done before going to Durham. By way of explaining that when the pathologist had pegged the earliest time at 10 a.m., Cooper asked "If he could be wrong three hours one way, why couldn't he be wrong three hours the other way?" This argument misstated and willfully misinterpreted Dr. Rodman's evidence.

Furthermore, Cooper said, Frank could have returned to Chapel Hill on two occasions on Dec. 24. Young's account doesn't say when those two times were. Finally, Cooper says that no one sees Frank after 12:10 p.m. that day. This, too, seems a misstatement of evidence.

It would have taken at least 20 minutes to drive one way between Durham and Chapel Hill in December 1963. Were there really two times when Frank could have driven Stan's car back to the apartment, committed a sloppy murder and then to Durham again? It's somewhere between doubtful and impossible.

Frank's apartment was only two blocks from Huggins Hardware, and the store had a back door. If Olga Hackett could have been clearer about the time when she saw Frank, Cooper would not have been able to offer this possibility to the jury. But refer back to the timeline: She was probably too busy to be aware of the time. What she was sure of was that she saw Frank in the store on Christmas Eve.

Mr. Cooper ended by showing the jury a color photograph of Lucille's bloody and beaten face. "It would take someone with those objectives [Perry Young's parenthetical addition: "insurance, homosexuality"] in mind to destroy a face that way." Mr. Cooper wanted the jury to see Frank Rinaldi as someone not like them, as a man who did not live as they did.

Judge Mallard instructed the jury on the law and their duty. He reviewed the evidence, including a detailed recital of the timeline. He read from state statutes to explain circumstantial evidence.

Then he told the jury to ask itself these questions:

"Did Lucille Rinaldi die as a direct result of Frank Rinaldi's holding a pillow over her nose?

"Did she die as a result of Frank Rinaldi's tying a scarf around her head?

"Was the slaying done intentionally and with a fixed purpose and intent?

"Was it done willfully, deliberately and premeditated malice and aforethought?

"If you find the answer "yes" to all of these questions, then he is guilty. But if you have a reasonable doubt as to either of them, then it is your duty to acquit him."

Both defense and prosecution spoke with passion, with strong language
and Biblical quotations. Together, their closing statements took three hours. The judge's charge to the jury took two hours. It must have been a mentally and emotionally exhausting day for everyone.

The jury began to deliberate at 4:09 p.m. on Tuesday, Nov.17, 1964. They took a dinner break and then worked until 10 p.m. They resumed the next morning at 9:30 a.m. and came back with the verdict at 12:32 p.m. that afternoon.

Perry Young estimated that 120 people stayed in and around the courtroom as the jury deliberated that Tuesday night. They included reporters, law officers, court officials, attorneys, and friends and relatives of both Frank and Lucille. Young mentions that the mood was not somber, and that the Begg family passed the time by discussing North Carolina's alcohol beverage laws. No doubt, the spectators and participants experienced a sense of relief that the matter was now in the jury's hands. There were no more fights to fight, at least for a while.

When the jury came to its decision, it found Frank guilty. I did not and, to some degree, do not understand how and why they failed to find reasonable doubt. Could they answer yes to all of the judge's questions?

I've expressed my observations about why charges were filed and pursued against Frank when cooler heads should have prevailed. But a jury is different. It is made up of 12 individuals who cannot consider anything but the evidence they have heard and then must reach a unanimous decision. A jury will have its own sociology, its own dynamic and tension.

In an article in *The News of Orange County* (Hillsborough, NC), Thursday, Nov.19, 1964, the reporter said "The jury verdict was a surprise to most persons who'd followed the case." There was a juror, Mr. Walter Allison, who was apparently eager to talk to anyone who listened. Allison was a retired salesman from Hillsborough.

Allison said that when the jury went home at 10 Tuesday night, the vote was ten to two for acquittal. By noon on Wednesday, there was a unanimous vote to convict.

There were people who believed Frank was guilty in 1963 when the murder occurred and there are people who believe today that he was guilty. I think those people decide first that he committed the murder and then figure out how to shape the evidence to support that decision.

The first obstacle to a guilty verdict has to be all of the witnesses who place Frank and Stan Forte in Durham or Eastgate or on Franklin Street during the time Lucille died—between 10 a.m. and noon. The way to clear that obstacle is to disregard the pathologist's testimony. Cooper, in his closing argument, provided the way to do that. "If he could be wrong three hours one way, why couldn't he be wrong three hours the other way?" He discredited the scientifically established time of death.

The doctor was not "wrong." He testified ungracefully and later clarified.

But for the jury, accepting the idea that the pathologist could be wrong was a way out. They did not have to deal with the alibi witnesses at all.

VERDICT TURNED ON TIME OF DEATH. This was the headline for Perry Young's article in *The Chapel Hill (NC) Weekly*, Sunday Nov. 22, 1964. Young had held a lengthy interview with a juror he did not identify at the time. The juror said that, indeed, one of the two jurors who initially voted to convict made the point with emphasis that Dr. Rodman was only human and could be wrong. It also seems that jury to some degree disregarded noon as the latest time Lucille could have died. They picked up on 2, a time never mentioned in testimony, but which Cooper used in his closing argument. Closing arguments are not evidentiary, but jurors—individually or collectively—may have a hard time remembering that, especially if it suits a purpose.

Young quoted Dr. Rodman as saying, "I would have thought that would have been clear from my testimony. The 10 a.m. time limit was based on body temperature, and so was the 5 p.m. limit. Whereas the 12 noon limit was based on rigor mortis. All I was doing was showing the two extremes on the basis of body temperatures. It seems pretty obvious that the 5 p.m. extreme was absurd."

It was absurd, but it also opened the rest of Dr. Rodman's presentation to question. Perhaps he overestimated the jury's ability to make the distinctions he had made. When Cooper turned time of death into a sliding scale that could move either way, there was no opportunity for anyone to contradict him or clarify the jury's understanding.

When the jury began its work, a retired colonel, John Rogers, was elected foreman. A first vote was taken, with 10 to two in favor of acquittal. Rogers was one of the two.

There was then a general discussion, with people in favor of acquittal saying that the state had not proved guilt beyond a reasonable doubt. After a supper break, the jury began to review the case from the beginning.

They could not recall who had seen Frank and Stan first that Christmas Eve. They could not recall details about the stop the men had made at the Sunoco station, including the time of that stop. They returned to the courtroom and asked the judge to have testimony read back to them, but the judge refused the request.

Then came discussion of Dr. Rodman's testimony, the time of death and the sliding scale. The two in favor of conviction argued that the time of death could have been an hour or more earlier.

The jurors took another vote, this time it was eight for acquittal, four for conviction. The original two for conviction stood strong that they would not change their minds. There was some discussion of telling the judge that they were deadlocked, but the judge had already told them they could come back the next day, so they quit for the night.

On the first vote the next morning, there were seven for conviction and five for acquittal. Perry Young's juror said that the people in favor of conviction were the most persuasive. As a group, the jury continued to discuss details of the case, including the police work and its flaws including failure to check doors and windows and failure to immediately find more than $200 that was hidden in Lucille's purse; ultimately, they decided that the case didn't rest on the police work. They also decided they could believe Stan Forte's account of the day, but not his account of Frank's incoherence upon finding Lucille. Instead, they accepted Capt. Coy Durham's account of how calm Frank was as he sat at the dining room table in the apartment and answered Durham's questions; if he could be that calm, then he could have been calm enough to kill his wife and then go buy Christmas presents for her.

From the juror's comments on Eddie Gorman, it seems that the jury set his testimony about what Frank said to him at Eastgate aside.

Some jurors were not comfortable with circumstantial evidence, so, Perry Young wrote, they discussed the chain of events. "The chain of circumstances included 'the kind of person' Rinaldi was, his preoccupation with insurance, his relationship with his wife, and that he had tried to hire somebody to kill her."

In the 2003 *Independent Weekly* (Durham, NC) article, Mr. Young identified the juror he talked with as someone he had once worked with, someone he considered to be "good and decent." The juror confirmed that "the kind of man" Frank had been was something the jury discussed and took seriously. Cooper apparently knew his jury.

Another vote was taken and now only three voted for acquittal. Young's juror source said that people both focused on the three and tried not to pressure them. Two more came over to the conviction side. Walter Allison, the juror who was quoted in *The News of Orange County* (Hillsborough, NC), was the twelfth and last. Someone said to him, "And now, Mr. Allison, the monkey is on your back." No pressure?

It seems that Allison had two problems. He did not want to convict an innocent man to death, and he did not understand the judge's charge about circumstantial evidence. The latter point was discussed further, and he was reminded that guilty with the recommendation of a life sentence was one of the choices the jury had.

Mr. Allison changed his vote, and they had a verdict. After it was read, Frank was allowed a few minutes with his father, brother and uncle. Then he was taken to Central Prison in Raleigh.

My father believed that John Rogers swayed his fellow jurors by force of personality. Barry Winston says he and Gordon Battle made a mistake by letting Rogers serve. Rogers had experience with the military justice system and Frank's attorneys felt that with the prosecution's weak evidence, his experience would work in their favor. It turned out to be the opposite.

There was a strange incident late in the first trial. Two lawyers not associated with the case came into the courtroom and told the judge that Rogers had been overheard talking about the case in a restaurant. The judge did not allow that information to be presented to the jury, nor did he pursue it. It could have been grounds for a mistrial, or at least for replacing Col. Rogers with an alternate.

THE SECOND TRIAL, ordered by the state Supreme Court, began on Oct. 11, 1965. Between the first verdict and the second trial, my father and Kevin Kerrane continued to support Frank and to believe in his innocence. They visited him whenever they could, wrote to him, sent books, and did what they could. Kerrane worked hard to raise money for a defense fund, writing to everyone who had ever known Frank, including classmates from Taft and Georgetown.

Barry Winston has told me that when Frank first hired him, he talked to a highly regarded defense attorney, Victor Bryant, about the defense. Gordon Battle then worked with Bryant and it was he who joined Winston. After the conviction, Bryant himself stepped into the case.

Frank's appeal contained several points having to do with decisions Judge Mallard had made. The N.C. Supreme Court ruled that one of them was sufficient for retrial: Judge Mallard should not have allowed prejudicial and incompetent testimony. That meant, he should not have allowed homosexuality to become an issue. Since ruling on that one issue was enough, the court did not comment on any of the others in the appeal.

JURY SELECTION for the second trial was not easy. On the first day, Oct. 11, five people were seated and 15 or more were challenged for cause; they had "unchangeable prejudiced opinions on the case," according to an article by Roland Giduz in the *Greensboro (NC) Daily News* on Oct. 12, 1965. Twenty-five of the original 96 people called to jury duty were left at the end of that first day.

It took 49 rejections before a sixth juror was seated the following day, but by the end of the next day, a jury was put together. There were eight men and four women. Nine were white and three were black. There were two alternates chosen, both women.

There was a different judge, George F. Fountain, a third defense attorney, and Cooper had an assistant; otherwise the principals were the same.

Testimony began on Thursday, Oct. 14. Captain Coy Durham testified first, followed by William Begg Jr. When Bill referred to Lucille's "rather unexpected" return home on Sept. 9, 1963, the defense objected to the characterization and the judge sustained the objection. The ruling put everyone on notice that this trial would be run differently.

The prosecution introduced evidence of a troubled marriage; the defense objected and the judge allowed some but not all of the testimony.

As in the first trial, there was testimony about Frank seeking loans in the fall of 1963 and about the issuance of the insurance policy on Lucille, a month before she and Frank were married.

In its Oct. 14, 1965 issue, the *News of Orange County* (Hillsborough, NC) ran an article with no byline, titled "Rinaldi's chances in new trial?" The writer suggested that, since the prosecution's case had been fully shown in the first trial, the defense's job should be easier this time. It was also said that testimony would be different because of the Supreme Court's ruling. On the other hand, the difficulty in seating a jury showed how strong and negative public opinion was toward Frank. Only one potential juror said he knew nothing about the case.

Eddie Gorman testified again, and gave the same testimony as before, though with an embellishment. Roland Giduz reported that he said "He wanted me to kill his wife, strangle her, choke her, make it look like rape—anything."

Gordon Battle went at Gorman on cross-examination, asking him if he was the killer: Had he gone to rob the apartment, found her there and killed her? He denied that, of course, but it is the defense's job to plant doubts and this was probably a more effective approach than was used in the first trial. Gorman did acknowledge that he did not go to the police—even though, according to him, Frank had asked him a dozen times or more to kill Lucille—until after he read about the murder in the newspaper.

What he did not repeat was what the Supreme Court had disallowed: He did not say that Frank made sexual advances.

The prosecution had lost its ability to use that particular innuendo but it also had new testimony to bring in. In the Saturday, Oct. 16, 1965 *Greensboro (NC) Daily News*, Roland Giduz reported on it. Chapel Hill police Sgt. James Farrell testified that he sat with Frank during the night of December 24-25, 1963, after the arrest. Frank said to the sergeant, "How can you stand to sit in the same room with me after what I've done?" or so the sergeant now recalled.

The defense tried hard to keep the jury from hearing this. Barry Winston took the stand himself to tell how he had asked the police not to question Frank in his absence.

As he tried to make his decision, Judge Fountain had the law officers reconstruct their investigation on the day and night of Dec. 24. SBI Agent Haywood Starling said he advised Frank that he did not have to talk to them and that if he did, his statements could be used against him. Starling questioned Frank at about 8:15 that night with Barry Winston present. He asked Frank whether or not he and Lucille had ever had problems and at that point, Winston took Frank into a private conference room. When they returned, Winston told the agent that there would be no more questioning that night.

The jury did not hear the arguments that lasted for four hours. In the end, the judge ruled that Frank's rights were not violated by introduction of things he said that night.

SBI Agent Frank Satterfield told the jury that Frank had talked to him, too, beginning at about 1 on Christmas morning. Frank had said that he supposed there were three motives for a murder like Lucille's: Money, financial difficulties and another woman. Sgt. Howard Pendergraph testified that Frank said something similar to him.

The defense made sure to have Agent Satterfield tell the jury that Frank denied killing Lucille.

Giduz wrote that prosecution witnesses gave answers on cross-examination grudgingly: Think of the way Lucille's letter was kept out of the first trial. And pause to wonder why was there no testimony in the first trial about what Frank said in the wee hours on Christmas morning.

Gordon Battle suggested to Sgt. Farrell that Frank said something like, "*If* I'm guilty of what I'm accused of, how can you stand to sit in the same room with me?" Farrell denied that he was altering or twisting Frank's words.

The letter Lucille wrote, dated, "on the Eve of" and signed, became a major topic of debate later that afternoon in the courtroom. The defense wanted it read into evidence, but the judge denied the request.

A sidebar: Walter Allison, the last of the first trial's jurors to come around to a guilty vote, attended the second trial and had to be cautioned not to talk to the new jury.

On Monday, Oct. 18, after calling 18 witnesses, the state rested.

In the second trial, when Dr. Rodman testified, he used a blackboard to make extensive notes about how he had determined the time of death. He explained to the jury that by using both body temperature and information about the degree of rigor mortis at the time the body was found, he could say that Lucille died no earlier than 10 that morning and no later than noon. He had said the same thing—although not smoothly—in the first trial and that jury had found a way to nullify his testimony.

For the defense, Stanley Forte told his familiar story in detail. He then had to withstand a long and aggressive cross-examination. The prosecution focused on the two life insurance policies from the perspective of the policy on Lucille being excessive. Giduz' article refers to the discrepancy in Frank and Lucille's income as if Frank earned more. At that point in their lives—with him in graduate school and teaching one course and her with a full-time job that paid what she considered to be a good salary—that doesn't seem to be true.

Once again, Solicitor Cooper brought out Frank's words, "Together again, baby," and asked the significance of the phrase. This time, Stan had an answer. He said it was a common expression in athletics, advertizing and show business. He went on to quote a baseball player from the recent 1965 World Series who had called a teammate "baby."

As in the first trial, Cooper asked Stan if he knew that Frank had been dismissed from the CIA for a security violation. Even though Cooper could not introduce homosexuality overtly this time, to suggest that a man was a security risk or dishonorable was to suggest he was gay. In the second trial, the defense was ready to counter the implication. They put into evidence proof that there was nothing dishonorable or unusual in Frank's separation from the CIA and that Frank had left of his own accord.

The defense called to the stand the parade of witnesses who had seen Stan and Frank together on Christmas Eve 1963 between 9 in the morning until after 1 in the afternoon.

The greatest difference in the defense's case was that Frank himself testified.

He denied that he killed Lucille. He denied saying things that the police officers and SBI agents testified to. One does wonder, if he had speculated to Agent Satterfield about motives for murder or had asked Sgt. Farrell how he could stand to sit in the same room with a murderer, why did the first jury not hear about it?

When asked whether he had told Agent Satterfield about having seen a psychiatrist, Frank said he had not. He did acknowledge that he had seen a psychiatrist at UNC for 14 or 15 sessions.

Cooper asked Frank if Lucille had given him money before they married. Frank said yes and agreed that it could have been as much as $700. Cooper questioned Frank about getting Stan

Forte to cash Lucille's checks for him. Frank said that was true. There were other questions about finances—all aimed at creating a sense that Frank had a financial motive for killing his wife.

Perry Young had moved on from *The Chapel Hill Weekly* (and went on to a long and important career as a writer using his full name, Perry Deane Young). A reporter for the *Charlotte Observer,* J.A.C. Dunn, wrote the kind of long and detailed stories about the second trial that Young had written about the first. Dunn had previously worked at *The Chapel Hill Weekly.* That paper carried his articles from the *Charlotte (NC) Observer.*

Dunn reported that Cooper wanted to have the postal inspector testify again—as in the first trial—about an investigation of material Stan Forte had received by mail. The defense protested. The jury was excused and the matter was debated. Cooper wanted to use the inspector to impeach Stan's testimony. The judge ruled that it was irrelevant, so it was not heard.

Dunn also wrote that Cooper asked Frank about his expertise about movies. Frank was in fact more than knowledgeable about movies, theater and Hollywood. The subject of his dissertation at UNC was playwright Philip Barry who wrote for the stage and the movies. Cooper zeroed in on the movie, "A Place in the Sun." Frank had seen the movie a number of times. Cooper asked him, "Didn't the theme of that film center on a man murdering his wife?" Frank pointed out that a subtheme is "the unfairness of prosecution staffs and planted evidence."

None of the reports I have read explained how Lucille's final letter was at long last put into evidence, but it was once the prosecution stipulated that it was in her handwriting. When I asked Barry Winston why the letter was finally allowed in, his answer was that the second judge was more reasonable than the first.

The letter was read aloud in court on Tuesday, Oct. 19. It was addressed to Kevin Kerrane. Frank broke down in tears upon hearing it.

Kerrane testified for the defense. He told the jury about the bathroom window with no lock on it, and he told about Eddie Gorman having had a key when he cleaned the apartment five or six months earlier. The prosecutor asked Kevin if he had told the police about these facts, and Kevin said that he had informed Agent Satterfield and the Chapel Hill officer who had questioned him early in 1964. In rebuttal, the solicitor called Agent Satterfield and the officer back to the stand. They both denied that Kerrane had told them about Eddie and the key.

Kevin saw Agent Satterfield in the corridor later and asked him why he had lied. Satterfield's answer was, "Oh, you know Rinaldi's guilty."

A number of character witnesses, including my father, were called to attest for Frank.

By noon on Wednesday, Oct. 20, 1965, both prosecution and defense rested.

Cooper's assistant solicitor, Robert Satterfield, presented the first part of the prosecution's closing. Dunn reported that Satterfield talked for half an hour.

Gordon Battle began dismantling the prosecution's case and as he finished his presentation, he read Lucille's letter again and said, "Nothing can bring back Lucille or the baby, but we can tell Frank Rinaldi he is free to go out and pick up the crumbled and shattered pieces of his life ..."

Barry Winston spoke for half an hour.

AT 4:10 THAT AFTERNOON, VICTOR BRYANT began his closing statement. Dunn described him as an old-fashioned orator, elderly, with a soft voice and with the ability to fix the courtroom on himself and his words. He also read the words from Lucille's letter, "Frank has kissed and smiled his kisses and smiled and departed for Durham to tell Santa what a good girl I am."

Bryant also used an unattractive ploy. He suggested that the Begg family wanted to collect the $40,000 in life insurance. It brought gasps, according to Dunn, and caused Clara Begg to cry. It wasn't a pretty thing to say, but Bryant might have responded that the Beggs had said some ugly things, too, without any greater support for their testimony.

Cooper gave his closing the next day at 9:35 a.m. He spoke for more than an hour and decried Bryant's attack on the Begg family. He made his argument based on Eddie Gorman's testimony and Frank's financial situation.

Judge Fountain spent an hour and a half reviewing evidence for the jury and instructing them on how to apply evidence. He gave them a lunch break and then added to his charge: He explained the legal definition of an alibi and reminded the jury that Frank had claimed to have an alibi.

The jury had three verdicts to choose from: Guilty of first-degree murder, guilty of second degree murder, and not guilty.

THE JURY BEGAN TO DELIBERATE at 2:05 p.m. on Thursday, Oct. 21, 1965. The reporters who covered the second trial all contributed to the sense that it was a tense and hard-fought trial. None of the lawyers seem to have suffered a letdown in the 11 months since the first trial. They worked hard and gave it all they had.

Dunn gave lively descriptions of the atmosphere in and around the courtroom while the jury deliberated. Lawyers argued a point again, until someone said it no longer mattered. Some people paced. Bryant, an opera fan, talked opera in the back of the room. My father chatted with Frank and his family. The jury was located in a room above the courtroom, and sounds from the room could be heard.

At about 10 p.m., the jury sent for coffee and indicated that they wanted to work longer. They did reach a verdict that night, after a total of eight hours and 40 minutes. Not guilty.

Frank Rinaldi, his brother, father and uncle wept and embraced. Friends and supporters cheered the jury. Frank found a telephone and called his mother. He thanked his lawyers and jury. He did not have kind words for the press, blaming coverage of the case for the 99 potential jurors who were dismissed for cause, for having made up their minds in a way that could not be changed.

Mr. Bryant acknowledged Frank's friends for standing with him.

The foreman of the jury, Donald Stewart, gave interviews about the process of reaching a verdict. The jury used secret ballots and the first count was six to six. They reviewed the evidence and, from Stewart's account, focused on the time of death and the alibi witnesses. They took a total of five ballots to reach a unanimous verdict. Although minds were settled or changed, they seemed to find a process that prevented the monkey from being put on anyone's back.

It seems clear that the two people on the first jury who believed Frank was guilty, began with that perspective and then worked the evidence to fit it. They had the strength of personality to prevail. Perhaps the lawyering for the defense was crisper and sharper the second time around and perhaps the jurors' individual and collective characters were more inclined to look fairly and without prejudice at the evidence they had been given. Arguments such as "the kind of person" Frank was (or was labeled by the solicitor) did not penetrate this time.

Most importantly, the time of death and the alibi witnesses emerged from what Barry Winston called "red herrings, smoke screens and smears." If the simplest answer is most often correct, then the simple answer was indeed not guilty.

To the best of my knowledge, no efforts were made by the Chapel Hill police or the SBI to investigate Lucille's death after the second verdict.

⌒

I KNOW LITTLE about Frank's life after acquittal. Kevin Kerrane said that he was reclusive for a period of time, and that certainly is understandable. It is not hard to imagine that he was changed forever. He completed his Ph.D. at the University of Massachusetts. His obituary says that he retired as dean of Paeir College of Art in Connecticut. He lived in Waterbury with his parents in the house in which he was raised. His mother, Dora Christiano Rinaldi, died at age 103 in August 2009, just three months before Frank's own death.

My father described Frank as theatrical, my sister recalls. Kevin Kerrane told me that he could be flamboyant, and that he was generous and not at all physical, that he could be petulant, and that, although they had the usual sorts of fallings-out that roommates have, he never saw Frank angry. Barry Winston added such words as brilliant, sarcastic, irreverent. It is clear that Frank could inspire deep friendship and loyalty from those people who understood him. But he was probably not an easily accessible person, and that could and did go against him during his troubles.

Soon after Frank died in 2009, another Chapel Hill native, Charles Mann, revisited the murder and the trials on his website, Chapel Hill Memories. There were hundreds of responses, many of them from Rinaldi and Begg family members. Their pain was still fresh, 46 years after Lucille died. The 1963 loss of Lucille and the baby continues to devastate two families.

CHAPEL HILL AND THE UNIVERSITY HAVE SEEN MURDERS SINCE LUCILLE RINALDI'S. Most of them have been committed by acquaintances, family members and loved ones—as most murders are. But there are the random and the unsolved. In the summer of 1965, while Frank was in Central Prison, a student named Sue Ellen Evans was stabbed to death in Coker Arboretum on campus in the middle of the day. No one was ever charged.

Twenty-six year old Kristen Ann Lodge-Miller went for a morning jog in July 1993. She was attacked by 18 year old Anthony Simpson, who attempted to rape her before killing her. They were strangers to each other.

In January 1995, a law student named Wendell Williamson shot and killed two strangers on Franklin Street with an M-1 rifle. He was found not guilty by reason of insanity.

The president of the UNC student body, Eve Carson, was kidnapped, robbed and murdered by two strangers in 2008. Two young men were charged. Demario Atwater pled guilty to both state and federal charges and Laurence Lovette, Jr. was convicted in both court systems.

In the fall of 2012, a UNC student, Faith Danielle Hedgepeth, was murdered in her apartment. As I write, no one has been charged.

I believe that every community, whether judged to be safe or dangerous in some objective sense, will suffer from crimes that cut into its collective heart and threaten its sense of collective self. Those are crimes that people feel "cannot happen here." Lucille Rinaldi's death was such a crime, and for me, it happened when I was at an age to absorb its lessons. I love my hometown, but learned at an early age that it is not the ideal village people wanted it to be in 1963, and still do.

Sometime in the early 1990s, I told my father my theory that Frank was convicted because Chapel Hill could not endure Lucille's death going unsolved. Dad seldom showed anger, but he did then, "That's no reason to send an innocent man to prison." That flash of anger was as bright as it would have been 30 years earlier.

Whenever I hear that justice is for the victim of a crime, I say no. Justice must be for the accused. If it isn't, then any of us could go through Frank Rinaldi's ordeal. If we dare think "it cannot happen here," we set ourselves up to make a terrible mistake, and to do it with that most human of creations—the airtight rationalization. Too many innocents go to prison for no better reason than that.

❧

OF THE LESSONS I LEARNED FROM FRANK'S ORDEAL, I most cherish what my parents exemplified—how to stand with a friend in trouble.

If the two trials taught me to be skeptical of even the best of our institutions, they also taught me to remain hopeful.

As for me, I might have decided at 13 or 14 that I wanted to study law and become a defense attorney. That never tempted me, but the power of the Rinaldi story's arc lived on for me. A tiny bit of it became seed for my novel, *Until Proven: A Mystery in 2 Parts*, published in 2012. That work of fiction is not a recreation of Frank's experience, but of mine.

SOURCES

Conversation and email with Kevin Kerrane
Conversation with Barry Winston
Greensboro Daily News, Friday, December 27, 1963
    Byline, Roland Giduz
Durham Morning Herald, Thursday, Jan. 2, 1964
    Editorial
The News of Orange County, Thursday, Jan. 9, 1964
    No byline
The Chapel Hill Weekly, Wednesday, Nov. 11, 1964
    Byline, Perry Young
The Chapel Hill Weekly, Sunday, Nov. 15, 1964
    Byline, Perry Young
The Chapel Hill Weekly, Wednesday, Nov. 18, 1964
    Byline, Perry Young
The News of Orange County, Thursday, Nov. 19, 1964
    No byline
The Chapel Hill Weekly, Sunday, Nov. 22, 1964
    Byline, Perry Young
Greensboro Daily News, Tuesday, Oct. 12, 1965
    Byline, Roland Giduz
The Durham Sun, Wednesday, Oct. 13, 1965
    Byline, Roland Giduz
The Daily Tar Heel, Thursday, Oct. 14, 1965
    Byline, Ed Freakley
Unidentified paper
    Byline, Reese Hart
The News of Orange County, Oct. 14, 1965
    No byline
Greensboro Daily News, Friday, Oct. 15, 1965
    Byline, Roland Giduz
Greensboro Daily News, Saturday, Oct. 16, 1965
    Byline, Roland Giduz

Unidentified paper
  Byline, Roland Giduz
The Chapel Hill Weekly, Sunday, Oct. 17, 1965
  Byline, J.A.C. Dunn
The Durham Sun, Wednesday, Oct. 20, 1965
  Byline, Roland Giduz
The Chapel Hill Weekly, Wednesday, Oct. 20, 1965
  No byline
The Charlotte Observer, unknown date
  Byline, J.A.C. Dunn
The Durham Sun, Thursday, Oct. 21, 1965
  Byline, Reese Hart
The Charlotte Observer, Friday, Oct. 22, 1965
  Byline, J.A.C. Dunn
The Durham Sun, Friday, Oct. 22, 1965
  Byline, Reese Hart
Greensboro Daily News, Friday, Oct. 22, 1965
  No byline
Greensboro Daily News, Saturday, Oct. 23, 1965
  No byline
Charlotte Observer, Saturday, Oct. 23, 1965
  Byline, J.A.C. Dunn
The Chapel Hill Weekly, Sunday, Oct. 24, 1965
  Byline, not shown; probably J.A.C. Dunn
Unknown paper
  Byline, Lawrence Maddry
Two articles written after the Not Guilty verdict; clippings do
  not show dates; no bylines.
The Independent Weekly, August 13, 2003
  A Cautionary Tale for D.A. Jim Harden, by Perry Deane
  Young
www.chapelhillmemories.com